THE BATTLE FOR THE MIND

Learning to Think Like Christ

Kenneth W. Gilmore, Sr.

DEDICATION

I am delighted to dedicate this book to Ms. Dorothy Long. I want to thank you for your support and efforts to make the Lakefront family a warm, caring and dynamic Christian fellowship.

ACKNOWLEDGMENTS

A special thanks goes to my editor Diane Fischler who has been a faithful editor and friend.

A special thanks also to Len Campbell my graphic artist for giving me again the perfect look.

TABLE OF CONTENTS

"I know that nothing good dwells in me, that is my flesh, for the willing is present in me, but the doing of the good is not. For the good that I would, I do not do, but I practice the very evil that I do not want. If am doing the very thing that I do not want, I am no longer the one doing it, but it is sin that dwells in me. I find, then, the principle of the law of evil present in me. The one who wants to do good, I concur with the law of God in the inner man. I see a different law in the members of my body, waging war against the law of my mind, and making me a prisoner of the law of sin, which is in my member. Oh, wretched man that I am, who will set me free from this body of death? Thanks be to God through Jesus Christ, our Lord. So then, on the one hand, I myself with my mind am serving the law of God, but on the other, with my flesh, the law of sin."

—Romans 7:14

CHAPTER ONE

THE BATTLE FOR THE MIND

You are engaged in a spiritual warfare. It's not a warfare that's taking place on the fields of foreign soil. This is a spiritual war. It is a war for your mind and your allegiance between the power of evil and the power of good. Whomever your allegiance is to will determine whom you follow. You must be aware of how this battle takes place.

In Romans 7:14, the apostle Paul identified four laws:

The Law of God

The first law Paul mentions is the Law of God. The Law of God, is God's moral law; it tells mankind how they should live. The Law of God is righteous, spiritual, and holy. It reveals the holiness and the righteousness of God.

The Law of Sin

The second law Paul mentions is the Law of Sin, which is the principle that is contrary or opposite to the Law of God. This law is the governing principle that controls the flesh, that selfish independent will that opposes God's best for man. This law is under the control of Satan.

The Law of Your Mind

The third law Paul mentions is the Law of Your Mind. Your mind functions according to a law or principle in the conscious and the sub-conscious mind. Your mind is composed of intellect, will, and emotion. It is through these organs that man can think and analyze his actions. If the Law of God or the Law of Sin controls and dominates your thinking, your mind will function according to the Law of Sin. The Law of sin will wage war against the Law of your mind, making you a prisoner of the Law of Sin, which is in your member.

The Law of Your Members

The fourth law Paul mentions is the Law of Your Members. Your body functions according to the Law of Your Mind. Your mind is controlled either by God's will or Satan's will. The mind sends signals or messages to your members to carry out or fulfill the desired functions of your mind, which are controlled by God or Satan. There is a *constant* struggle in your mind between the Law of God and the law of sin that compels man to defy God and to live independent of His will.

Oh, wretched man that I am, who will set me free from this body of death?

Paul said that when you want to do that which is right, you find a law in your member that tells you what you should do. Or when your mind says this is the right thing to do, there's always a struggle that pulls you to go the opposite way.

Have you ever known anyone who has been addicted to any chemical substance abuse, once the monkey is on their back, they are forever a recovering alcoholic or a recovering drug addict. Why? Because the proclivity is always there to go the wrong way, even though one may have been sober five, ten or fifteen years.

If you do not allow the Word of God to control your life, you will find yourself in places that you never thought you would be. You'll find yourself doing things that you never thought you would do. Why? Because of the pull of the Law of Sin against your mind, telling your members what to do.

Your Belief System

A healthy Christian lifestyle is the result of a healthy Christian belief system. If what you believe about God and who you are not built upon a solid foundation, then your behavior will be unstable because your life is built on a shaky foundation. Your belief system determines your behavior. If you can change your belief system, you can change your behavior.

Your life as a Christian is directly related to what you believe about God and yourself. If your belief system tells you that you are no good, you will never measure up. If that's what you believe, that's how you will act. So, if you can change your belief system, you can change your behavior. That is called behavioral modification.

The Bible refers to this as the transformation of your mind or the renewing of your mind. But you need to understand that if you have an unhealthy belief system, you will have an unhealthy sense of self-worth.

When you came into this world you were born into a sinful environment. Your parents and schoolteachers cared about you, but they might have taught you values that may have been contrary to the Word of God.

Your belief system is based on what you've been taught. You operate off what you have been taught for ten, fifteen or twenty years. Then you came to Christ and surrendered your life to God. You still operate with the same old thinking and behavioral patterns. You continue to make the same mistakes repeatedly because you have retain the same bad thinking. It's because you keep thinking in that sinner mentality.

Your decision-making ability is based on old information that you use to evaluate and make decisions. If it doesn't sound right, you reject it. For many years, you've been accumulating old information in your subconscious mind; when you make decisions, you make them based on the values of that old information.

Do you ever wonder why physically abused women keep going back to the same old abuse? The reason why they return, even though they know that it's dangerous for them to go back, is because they have been conditioned, their minds have been programmed to think a certain way. I don't care how much you tell them, "You need to leave that abusive relationship." But they say, "No, I love him. He will change."

Remember, your belief system determines your behavior. Satan is battling to control your mind and ruin your life. Satan is busy putting negative patterns and worldly thoughts into your mind, which will produce negative, worldly behavior. When you tell Christians not to date non-believers, it's because their value system is not the same as yours. *"What does light have in common with darkness, or what do demons have in common with the Holy Spirit?"* (2 Corinthians 6:14)

Christians who rationalize and justify their decisions say, "Well, I can win him into the church. He treats me better than some of these guys in the church." If he's a non believer, even though you're trying to win him, Paul would say, "Don't date him until he's a firm believer in the faith." Paul said in 1 Timothy 3, *"If you're going to place a man in the position of an elder in the church, make sure that he's not a new convert. You need to put him to the test."* When a person is in love with you, they will say and do anything just to be with you. But when they have you, they will keep on doing what they used to do. The only contact you should have with pagans is to win them to Christ, and when they are fully in love with Jesus, then you can consider dating them.

The battle for the mind is a conflict between God's way, which is faith, and Satan's way of living by the desires of the world and the flesh. Some Christians are still living in the world. They still make decisions based on how the world thinks. Christians do not take ungodly advice from non-believers. Some are listening to satanic counsel. When you listen to the psychics, Tarot cards, Ouija boards, Horoscopes, that is satanic counseling.

God doesn't direct your life by the stars. He directs your life by His son. You must realize that the battle is between God's way faith and Satan's way, which is the flesh. You are the only one who can determine the winner in the battle for your mind. The battle for your mind is clearly seen in our scriptural text. Paul said, *"On one hand, I want to do this, for sin dwells in me."* And he said, *"When I want to do good, sin or evil is always present."* You want to do the right thing, then the devil raises his head. The devil, *he comes to steal, kill, and destroy.*

Many people have been westernized, that they do not believe in demons and angels, and really don't even believe in God. They may have a Sunday school affirmation that He's alive, but they do not live like God is really alive.

II Corinthians 4:1 says, *"We have this ministry and we receive mercy and we faint not, and renounce the hidden things of dishonesty. Not walking in craftiness! Nor handling the word of God deceitfully! But by the manifestation of the truth, we commend ourselves to every man's conscience in the sight of God. If our gospel be hid, it is hid to them that are lost, whom the god of this world has blinded the minds of them who believe not, lest the light of the glorious gospel who is the image of God shall shine in their heart"*

The devil blinds people's minds. Satan keeps them from seeing the truth because he knows that if they see the truth, they might just obey it. In John 8:44-45, Jesus says, *"You don't believe in me because you are the nature of your father. You are of your father the devil. And he walks not in the truth, because there is no truth in him. When he speaks a lie, he speaks of his own nature, for he is a liar."* Whenever you hear the devil speak to you, he is not telling you the truth! He may tell you a half-truth and you believe it, and you will discover that what you have are lies. Satan blinds people's minds from seeing the truth and he's the father of lies.

Strongholds

The first thing you need to know about the battle for your mind is that this battle is fought on the spiritual level. You cannot outsmart or outmuscle the devil. You must use the weapons of divine power if you're going to win the spiritual conflict.

In II Corinthians 10:3-5, Paul said, the main targets that must be destroyed in our lives are the strongholds in the mind. The devil may have some strongholds in your mind. You know what a stronghold is? A stronghold is a habit. You can't break it by yourself. *Although we walk in the flesh or we do not walk in the flesh. For the weapons of our warfare are not fleshly.* But these weapons are mighty through God, through the pulling down of strongholds. The only way you can pull down the habits of destructive behavior in your life you must have the power of God! " *Casting down every imagination, everything that exalts itself against the knowledge of God.*" He says you have to cast down imagination. You know where imagination comes from? Mark 7:15 says, that every thought comes from the heart. Jesus says, *"Evil thoughts, murders, adultery, fornication, all of that comes from the heart."* What you have to do is learn how to take control of your imagination. You know what imagination is? Imagination is a visual picture a mental picture. That's why Jesus said, in Matthew 5, *"Whosoever looks upon a woman and desires her, he's already committed adultery in his heart."* If you think about stealing something, it's already stolen. The Bible calls this covetousness. Jesus was interested in the spirit, not just the act itself. If you think it, if you say it, if you hate a person in your heart even though you never took a gun or knife, Jesus said you already committed murder. It begins in the heart. *Casting down imagination and every high thing that exalts itself.* Talking about pride!

John said, in I John 2:14, *Love not the world, neither the things in the world, they are the lust of the flesh, and the lust of their eyes, and the pride of life!"* You can get to the point where nobody can tell you anything. Proverbs 18 says, *"That pride goes before destruction! A haughty spirit before a fall."* When you can't be told anything, you are traveling a dangerous road. Bring into captivity every thought to the obedience of Christ. That's how the devil works. He will shoot you a thought into your mind. By the Word of God you have to get that thought out of your mind. You will start dwelling on that: "Well let me figure out, that if I do that, who is going to find out? How can I cover my tracks, keep people from finding out?"

You must learn to take captive every thought because a thought begins the whole entire process. In Proverbs 4:3, Solomon said,

"Keep your heart with all diligence, for out of it flows the issues of life." Take every thought captive to the obedience of Christ. You must pull down some strongholds. Bad patterns of thoughts are burned in your mind, either through repetition over time or through a one-time deeply shocking experience. If you do something over and over again, it becomes hard to break. I used to teach a class for the city of Tampa for people who wanted to stop smoking. People would chew gum, put the patch on, do everything and anything they could to stop.

But the principle I was teaching was to change their belief system. Some people have convinced themselves that they need a fix. Some people have convinced themselves they just need a man in their lives. But if you can control and change how you're thinking, you can change how you live.

You know why some people are in the ghetto? It isn't because they're down and out. Down and out means they can't work. But their minds have been conditioned over time.

I'm not against poor people, but I am against those who will not work.

How Strongholds Are Established in Your Mind

God designed you to live in fellowship with Him, and to fulfill His purpose here. But when you were born physically alive, you were born spiritually dead. You were born into a world that opposed God's system. Ephesians 2:1 says, *"By nature you are children of wrath."* So, what you do? You do according to your nature. A dog is created for a specific purpose. A dog or a cow acts in accordance with his nature.

God designed you to be in fellowship with Him but because of sin, you have a sinful nature and now you act according to the nature that's in you. That nature is controlled by the devil. Jesus said, *" You need to be born again. You need to be a new creature. Old things are passed away and behold all things have become new."* If you're a new creature, then you have a new nature, a new attitude, a new mind, and then you should think and act like your new nature.

The problem with the carnal Christian is that though he has been saved, he is not walking in an intimate relationship with God, and he is still thinking and acting like the old man. This is because his mind has not been reprogrammed to think and act like a Christian. A change has been brought into your life.

Before you came to Christ, all your experiences came from the sinful environment, which influenced and shaped you.. Notice the influences in your life: your parents, teachers, friends, and spouses have all influenced you. Places: your homes, schools, and camps have all influenced you. Books, magazines, newspapers all have influenced you. The television! Movies have influenced you to act and think more like the world than like God. Music! you listen to the wrong music and are influenced by the world how you think about love. How you think about sex. How you think about family and what you think about the opposite sex.

When you became a Christian, the old ways of thinking and behaving changed. You learned and adjusted your way of thinking to your new environment. No longer will you conform to this world, but you will be transformed by the renewing of your mind. Whenever you feel tempted to leave God's plan and purpose for your life, you are experiencing a temptation. Let me show you what temptation is.

What Is Temptation?

A temptation is a legitimate need that you have. But the problem with a temptation is that you're choosing to let the devil meet the need rather God. God recognizes that you need companionship. God recognizes that you need love. God recognizes that you need money. But to obtain any of those needs other than God's way is Satan's way. The purpose of temptation is to get you to fulfill genuine needs that you have through the world, through the flesh, through the devil. That's where the real battle is. Either you trust God to give it to you or Satan says, "I'll give it to you." That's what sin is. Sin is a matter of unbelief. You don't trust God to do what He's said He will do for you. So, many decide, "Well, I'm going to get it my own way. I don't trust God."

The devil has watched you all your life. He knows what your weaknesses are and he knows when to attack you. The devil is smart, he isn't a chump. He is not a neophyte. He's not somebody new at this thing. The devil has been sizing you up, and not only sizing you up but also setting you up. You have to be smart enough to know when you're walking into a trap. If it sounds too good to be true, it is. There's a hook somewhere in there.

I Corinthians 10:13 says, *"There is no temptation that has taken you that is not common to men. Every temptation that you're going through, somebody has already gone through it. God is faithful."* and in the midst of every temptation you have, know this, that God is faithful, God will stand by you, God will give you the strength and the ability to make it through every temptation. God is not going to put on you more than you can bear. Above and beyond all, God knows what your strengths and weaknesses are. With a temptation, He will always provide a way of escape so that you may be able to bear it.

In other words, God is not going to let Satan have an unfair advantage over you. You have to realize that the only way you are going to identify temptation is to be near God. When the Word of God says, God will meet all your needs and you go out looking for somebody else to meet your needs what are you doing? You're trusting in yourself rather than trusting in God.

The moment you are tempted to have your needs met by the world instead of Christ, you are on the threshold of a decision. If you don't immediately choose to take captive every thought, to make it obedient to Christ, you begin to consider the temptation as an option. You cannot say, "Well, I'll make a decision., I'll think about it." You cannot do that! If your mind is on the Word of God, the indwelling presence of the Holy Spirit in your life, then when sin tempts you, immediately take the thought and reject it. When Jesus was tempted by the devil, do you know how He was victorious? He quoted the word. He said, *"Man shall not live by bread alone, but by every word that proceeds out of the mouth of God."* That's how He was victorious. Jesus knew that, legitimately, to have His needs met, He had to have them met by God. Because everything the devil offers you, it has a hook in it.

In order to win the battle for your mind, you must have a plan. If your mind has been programmed wrong, it can be reprogrammed by listening to and studying the Word of God. You can win, but you must choose the right way. All of us are products of our decisions. You will reap the consequences of those choices you have made, whether they are good or whether they are bad.

Which one will you allow to have control over your life God or Satan? The devil has had a stronghold in your life for too long. Now is the time to ask God to help you remove that stronghold in your life. Whatever it is!

"Sanctify Christ as Lord in your hearts, be ready to make a defense to everyone who asks you to give an account for the hope that is in you, yet with gentleness and with reverence. Keep a good conscience so that, in the things in which you are slandered, those who revile your good behavior in Christ will be put to shame. For it is verily, if God should will it, so that you suffer for doing what is right rather than doing wrong."

—1 Peter 3:15

CHAPTER TWO

YOUR BELIEF SYSTEM

There is a spiritual conflict taking place in the spiritual realm. It is a conflict or war between God and Satan and that war has been determined, ultimately, by the work of God through the work of Christ on the cross. But that doesn't minimize the fact that the devil is still interested in trying to destroy everyone with him and to deceive you with falsehoods.

II Corinthians 4 says, *"Satan is the god of this world system, and he blinds the minds of those to keep them from obeying the truth. "* The only way you can determine what is true is that you must read the Word of God. This battle exists between the forces of righteousness and the forces of evil.

Your belief system is like a missile that has

a hidden radar. That missile is guided by a computer system. The missile is moving toward its predetermined target. A belief system is a set of presuppositions. All of us operate off a set of principles that we assume to be true or not true. Let me give you a good example. Back in the 1400s before Christopher Columbus ever sailed across the Atlantic, everybody believed that the world was flat. So, no explorers were willing to go beyond Spain's shores because they believed if they went too far, they would fall off the planet. That was a set of beliefs. Now, when Christopher Columbus sailed beyond Spain, he disproved that principle. Once he sailed across the Atlantic ocean and showed the royal court the spoils that he brought back, they were convinced that the world was no longer flat. In May1961, John F. Kennedy said that "We would put a man on the moon." But there were some people who believed that was impossible. So, whatever your beliefs are, they determine how you look at the world. Your beliefs determine how you will act.

Whatever you believe, it determines your behavior. If you say that you are not beautiful or handsome, I don't care what anyone tells you, you are not going to believe it because you've been conditioned to look at things differently. In Carter G. Woodson's book, *The Miseducation of the Negro*, he said that if you have told a man for years that he never could enter the front door, he always had to go to the back of the house. That's what he was use to. If you have been trained and conditioned for so long, and someone says to him, "Now, you can go to the front door," because his mind has been conditioned, he will still go to the back door. When he gets there, he discovers that there is no back door, so he will dig a hole.

The National Negro College fund has a theme, *"A mind is a terrible thing to waste."* Whoever controls your mind, controls you. So, you hold a number of beliefs that you accept as true. These presuppositions are necessary if you are to think at all. Once a person commits himself to a set of presuppositions, his direction and his destination are already pre-determined.

What Makes Up a Person's Belief System?

There are three points you need to know about a belief system. First, everyone has a belief or a belief system. Everybody has a *modus operandi, that is,* how you function.

Second, if you want to know what a person's belief system is, first ask him what he thinks about God. Even among God's people, we do not all share the same beliefs about God.

There are people who believe, for example, that there is no God. If they believe that there is no God, there is no point in talking to them about the Bible. Why? Because they don't believe in the Bible. You have to convince them some other way that the reason why you believe in God is not just simply based on the Bible because your beliefs are based on some other considerations.

Some people are agnostics. They say, "There isn't enough information for me to believe one way or the other. My belief is suspended. You can't make a decision one way or another." You meet people who say, "I'm not anything." Peter said in I Peter 3:15, *"you have to be ready to give an answer to every man that asks for the reason."* There are reasons for why you believe what you believe. If you don't know the reason why, then you do not know what you believe. Then the devil comes along and he'll be able to destroy your faith.

Thirdly, reality. I would contend that most people live only for the here and now. They live only for what they can see. They don't live their lives with any expectations that God may come at any moment. They believe only in what they can see.

Christians believes that beyond this reality we experience another world. Solomon, in the book of Ecclesiastes, warns the man who chooses not to worship God that he is foolish. The reason why he is foolish is because he never looks beyond the sun. There's another world beyond the sun. Even though you cannot see it with your natural eye, it doesn't mean that it does not exist.

There are a lot of things you can't see, but it does not mean that they are not true. Do you see the radio or television waves passing through the air, You can't see those invisible waves. But systems operate based on radio waves that are passing through the air. You believe in something. It may not be what I believe, but you believe in something. You go to the physician because you believe that the physician has been trained to understand the physical body.

Therefore you are trust his diagnosis because you believe in the education and the training he has received. Have you ever gone to the physician and he has given you a prescription and you couldn't read what it said? You took that prescription to the pharmacist and didn't know whether or not the pharmacist could read it, because some people have received the wrong medicine based on what they believe is right.

But your belief in the doctor and in the pharmacist is not blind faith because they have training and they have demonstrated to you that they are consistent and that 99.99 percent of the time they give you the correct information. All of us operate off 99.9 percent information.

When parenting tests are conducted to determine the blood type of a person, the statistical probability is always 99.9 percent So, the preponderance of the evidence says that it's your child. In a court of law, there is no such thing as 100 percent evidence.

Two people can see the same accident and come up with different interpretations. That's why people are convicted on what they call preponderance of the evidence. What's the preponderance of the evidence? The evidence is so heavily against you that you've got to be the one. There have been people who have been convicted by circumstantial evidence even though they may be innocent. But in a court of law, they operate on a preponderance of the evidence. So, when I talk to people who say they don't believe in the Bible, my question to them is, what standard of proof are you using?

Don't be unfair to those who are believers because they believe in the Bible. Christians did not throw away their brains. They did not throw away their minds when they decided to believe in the gospel— that Jesus is the Son of God.

Peter said, be ready to give an answer to every man for the hope that is within you. Can you give people answers as to why you believe what you believe? Before you can even start communicating to people, you have to answer, "How do you know the Bible is true?" There is much information that you assume to be true.

For example, you have never met the first president of the United States. What you know is what you are told. You believe in Socrates and Plato, and Socrates never wrote anything. What is known about Socrates is based on what Plato wrote.

CHAPTER THREE

BIBLICAL
CHARACTERISTICS
OF AN
UNSAVED MIND

The battle for the mind is a battle that exists between the forces of righteousness and the forces of evil, that is, God and Satan, and your mind is neutral. Your mind is neutral, and whichever power controls your mind it will control you.

Ephesians 2:1, says *"And you were dead in your trespassing and your sin. And which you formerly walked according to the course of this world, according to the prince and power of the air, of the spirit that is now working in the sons of disobedience. Among them we too all formerly live, in the lust of our flesh, indulging the desires of the flesh and of the mind. And by nature, children of wrath, even as the rest."* Paul described the unsaved man.

If you want to know what an unsaved mind

looks like, talk about people being lost. I want you to know what condition the unsaved mind is in. Man is a triune being. He is made up of body, soul, and spirit. The body has five senses.

The five senses are hearing, smelling, tasting, feeling, and touching. So, the only way that the mind knows anything is through the five senses. The soul is the mind; it's the personality. The five senses send information to the brain, or to your mind, and then your mind tells the other members of the body what to do.

Paul said we are made up of body, soul, and spirit. Your mind is neutral. Therefore, the warfare going on in your mind is between the law of God, righteousness, and the law of sin. Whichever one of these laws wins, you will decide to obey, the law of your mind to the law of God. Then the law of God is going to produce righteousness in your body.

In Mark 7:15, your heart is your mind. You don't need to waste your mind, but you need to fill your mind with good thoughts. *What comes out of a man, is that which defiles a man from within comes out of his heart proceed evil thoughts. Adultery, fornication, murder, theft, covetousness, wickedness.* All of which come from the heart. So, if your heart can be changed, your belief system can change your behavior.

As far as God is concerned, God looks at the unsaved mind and it is shocking what He sees. Genesis 6:5 says that *"God repented that He ever made man, because man's imagination was wicked before God and decided that He was going to destroy the world because of the wickedness of men."* Their minds had become vain; their minds had become corrupt.

In Romans 1, Paul said, *"I'm not ashamed of the Gospel of Christ, for it is the power of God unto salvation, unto anyone who believes it. To the Jew first and also unto the Greek, for therein is the righteousness of God revealed from faith unto faith. For the just shall live by faith."*

The gospel contains the condemnation and the wrath of God. But the gentile who does not know God based on the revealed law of God written in the Ten Commandments, he does know about God through creation. He has a law written on his heart.

But he refuses to acknowledge God as God; therefore God gives man over to a reprobate mind, Which is a depraved mind. It's a mind that is twisted and distorted. It's a mind that has been totally wrung. It's nothing but evil. Paul said that when God gives you over to a reprobate mind, you are subject to do anything.

The law of God, to the Jew, was the Ten Commandments. But the law of God revealed to the gentile was by nature. God put something in his heart and his conscience to let him know the difference between right and wrong. So, if you choose not to acknowledge that God exists, then the next act you will do is to disregard the law of God.

It'll be like the old wild, wild West. When everybody had a gun. That was the law. Every man was a law unto himself. In the book of Judges, after God has rescued Israel, and brought the Israelites out of Egypt, God raised up judges to protect the nation of Israel. After they were protected, they would go into apostasy, into rebellion. *Every man did what was right in his own eyes.*

When you don't have God in your life and you move away from the law of God, everything is up for grabs. Romans 1, when you move away from God, you're moving to idolatry. "You begin to worship four-footed beasts, birds and reptiles and everything else."

In America, we don't worship beasts or reptiles and creatures like that; we worship our cars and our houses. Materialism has become our God. When you leave idolatry, your next practice is sexual perversion.

Romans 1 says that you change the natural function of the man for the woman, men with men and women with women. We have a society that wants to endorse and promulgate homosexuality and lesbianism. The Bible says it's a sin!

But all of it stems from the fact that a

person doesn't know the God of the Bible. If you're not careful, you can drift and drift away from God, and then you'll reach a point of no return. You can't get back.

The unsaved man's mind is evil; his thoughts and imagination are evil. God repented that He ever made man. Man's mind is depraved; he has chosen not to worship God and not to honor Him, and it has led him into spiritual idolatry and sexual immorality to the extent that he has exchanged the natural use of a woman for a man. Man has been given over to a reprobate mind. His mind does not have the critical capacity to reason between right and wrong.

In II Thessalonians 2:1, *"Consider the Lord Jesus Christ and our gathering together with him. Not to be soon shaken in mind or troubled neither by spirit, neither by the word, nor by the letter. And though the day of Christ is at hand."*

In verse 9, *"And the coming of the lawless one is according to the working of Satan. With all power and signs and wonders. With all unrighteousness, deception among those who perish, because they do not receive the love of the truth, that they might be saved! For this reason God will send them strong delusion to make them believe a lie when they should believe the truth."* God will keep on sending the truth, and the unbeliever will keep on rejecting it. Then God gets to the point when He will not send any more truth because the unbeliever does not want to hear it. Like the pagan gentiles in Romans 1, *"They suppressed the truth."*

God can keep sending you truth and you keep on rejecting it. God says, "Well, I'll tell you what. They do not want to hear the truth, I'm just going *"To send them a lying spirit to make them believe a lie when they should obey the truth."* God gives all of us free moral choices. We are a product of our choices.

God always is the one that pre-arranges and presents the consequences. What you sow, that is, choice, you will reap. People will sow wild oats and then they pray to God for a crop failure. Solomon says the way of the transgressor is hard. So you keep living, you keep going down that path of futility. God keeps trying to give you signals, give you warnings, and you refuse.

In Hebrews 2:1, it says, *"Therefore, we must give more earnest heed to the things that you hear, least we let them drift away."* If the word was spoken by angels and proved steadfast, and every transgression and disobedience received a just reward, how shall we escape if we neglect so great our salvation?* You can't escape.

Ephesians 4:17-18 says that the unsaved man's mind is darkened and vain. In other words, he sits around and thinks about doing evil. In the book of Proverbs 6, the wise man Solomon said that there are people who sit around and think about nothing but how to conjure up evil and how to set traps for other people. Their minds are darkened and vain.

In Romans 8:6, the mind of the unsaved man is at war between God and himself. In other words, he's so angry with God and God is angry with him that the judgment and the wrath of God are coming upon the sons of disobedience.

Why? Because man refuses to surrender to God's way and he wants to go his own way. And God says, because you go your own way, I'm going to damn you. He's at war. A man who doesn't know God and refuses to acknowledge God he is at war not only with God but he is at war with himself. He can't find peace. He goes to the liquor bottle; he can't find peace in the liquor bottle. He goes to the drug dealer and he can't find peace in marijuana, so he tries to go to the next level, heroin, coke. Still can he find peace.

People try to find answers to life in their careers. What they can't find, they keep jumping from job to job. Or they look for happiness in a man, so they jump from man to man or jump from woman to woman. They can't find joy. They can't find satisfaction. You cannot find it in anyone but Jesus.

Titus 1:15 says that the mind of the unsaved man is defiled. All he thinks about is garbage, filth, pollution, contamination. He just sits up and has his mind on filth. You know the old saying that an idle mind is a devil's workshop? II Corinthians 10:3-4 says *"You must take every thought captive to the obedience of Christ."* You know how the devil wins. He shoots a thought in your mind. You'll be on your knees praying, and the devil just shoots a thought. If you don't immediately take that thought captive, you know what you will do? You start considering that temptation as an option.

Temptation is any legitimate need you have, but you choose to have that need by the world or by Satan rather than God. That's what temptation is. I Corinthians 10:13 says that *" there is no temptation that has overtaken you that is not common."* Every temptation that you have is common to everybody. Some people either have gone through it, are going through it, or they will go through it. John 2:15 says, *"love not the world neither the things of the world, for the lust of the eyes, the lust of the flesh is the pride of life.*

Hebrews 2:14 says that *"Jesus was tempted at all points, like you are, yet without sin. In the midst of your temptation,"* God is faithful. He will not allow you to be tempted beyond what you are able if you're going through trials or a temptation. He will not leave you by yourself. He's there. You must feel His presence.

Do You Know What a Stronghold Is?

The devil has come in and he has set up camp in your life and it is difficult to get him out. Don't give any place to the devil. Give him a foot, he'll take a yard. That's why it's dangerous to fool around with sin. The devil shoots a thought in your mind, and he will use your imagination and fantasy. You know what fantasy is? You're sitting there imagining. You started reflecting about what you used to do and where you used to go, and that fantasy is real.

In I Timothy 6:5, the unsaved man's mind is corrupt. In Ephesians 2:1, *"You are dead in your trespasses and your sins." And whence you once walked according to the course of this age or according to this world.*

What the world did, that's what you did. Whatever fad came along, you got caught up in it. Christians should be counter-cultured, they should be different.

They should set a standard of excellence. *"According to the prince and the power of the air,"* not only are you controlled by what goes on in the environment, but you're also controlled by Satan! He's the one who ultimately pulls the strings in your life because your mind has been programmed to think and act a certain way—the conscious and the subconscious mind.

Many who became Christian gained much knowledge from their parents, teachers, environment, and from their peers. The choices you make are based on information that you are given, perhaps wrong. What God tries to do with you in terms of your mind, He tries to reprogram your mind, tries to get you to think like Christ.

Do not make your decisions based on the flesh and how you feel, but make your decisions based on righteousness. So when somebody calls you and starts gossiping on the phone, hang the phone up nicely.

People will not understand you. They will say, that you think you are better than they are, but you do not have time to fill your mind up with junk. In Proverbs 4:23, Solomon said, *"Guard your heart with all purity, for out of it flows the issues of life."* You let other people talk to you and put you up to doing evil but you have to learn to tune out this kind of temptation. Because if you hear it, you're going to start acting on it.

In I Corinthians 2:14, the apostle Paul said that the mind of the old man, the sinner, is programmed according to the world. *"The things of God are foolish to him; he cannot comprehend the things of the Spirit."*

He is ruled by his sense mechanisms, only what he sees, tastes, touches, and smells – these are the only things that are real to him! II Corinthians 4:4 says, *"Therefore since we have this ministry, we have received mercy and we faint not. We have renounced the hidden things of dishonesty. Not walking in craftiness, not handling the word of God deceitfully. But the manifestations of the truth, commending ourselves to every man's conscience in the sight of God. If our gospel is hid, it is hid to them that are lost or perishing. Whom the god of this world has blinded!"* Satan will blind your mind. In II Corinthians 11:2 says, *"I am jealous over you with godly jealously. For I have betrothed you to one husband that I may present you as a chaste virgin unto Christ. I fear that somehow Satan has deceived you by his craftiness, so that your mind may be corrupted from the simplicity that is in Christ."*

Did you know that the gospel is so simple? But you know what the devil has done? The devil has made life so complicated. In the religious world, we're trying to figure out which church to attend.

There are so many denominations — Baptist, Methodist, Presbyterian. We should have the same beliefs (I Corinthians 14:35). So, religious division is caused by the devil. How do I know that? *For he who comes to you and preaches to you another Jesus.*

There are people preaching another Jesus. They are not preaching the Jesus of the Bible. *If you receive a different spirit.* These false teachers proclaim a different Holy Spirit, not like the Holy Spirit that I read about in my Bible. *If you receive a different gospel.*

There are people who are preaching a different kind of good news than I'm preaching. And Paul said it in Galatians 1:7-8, *"Though we are an angel preaching another gospel unto you, let him be accursed."* He's under the judgment of God. Everybody who preaches is not preaching the gospel.

For those who says they have the Holy Spirit, I want to ask them, What kind of spirit do you have? Because John said in I John 4:1, *"Test and try the spirits. For many false prophets have gone out into the world. False prophets, deceitful workers, transforming themselves into the apostles of Christ. Satan himself transforms himself into an angel of light. Therefore, it is no great thing his ministers also transform themselves into ministers of righteousness. Satan has his own minis-*

ters." If Satan has his own gospel, his own Jesus, his own Holy Spirit, it just makes sense he'd have his own church.

The Flesh Versus the Spirit

Galatians 5:17 says, *"For the flesh lusts against the spirit, and the spirit against the flesh."* The flesh has to do with your fallen nature. The flesh has to do with your fallen desire, those desires that are against the will of God.

The Spirit consist of those things that please God, and so there is a conflict of warfare between the flesh and the Spirit. These are contrary to one another. If you are led by the Spirit, you are not under the law. The works of the flesh are evident.

There are people who have committed all kinds of sexual sin, whether it's sodomy or whether it's lesbianism or homosexuality; it's called fornication and unclean. There are people who are just unclean and unhealthy.

Lewd

You know what lewdness is? It's when people do not care; they have no public decency about themselves.

Idolatry

Idolatry has to do with the worship idols. In Jeremiah 10, God condemns Israel because of the sin of idolatry. The foolishness of idolatry. *"Hear the word which the Lord spoke of the house of Israel. Thus says the Lord, do not learn the way of the gentiles. Do not be dismayed as signs of heaven, for the gentiles are dismayed at them. The customs of the people are foolish, for one goes into the forest and cuts down a tree. They decorate that tree with silver and gold."*

That's the foolishness of idolatry. They go into the woods and cut down a tree and then they take precious gold and silver put it on the tree. Then they fall down and worship it. They fastened that tree with nails and hammers so that it will not topple. It's upright! Like a palm tree.

The New American Standard says it's a scarecrow in the field. You know what a scarecrow is? It can't speak, it is full of straw. It's supposed to scare away the birds, but "I've seen crows sitting on tops of scarecrows."

They're supposed to scare away birds, to keep them from eating the harvest. The problem with idolatry is you're the one creating it. If you created something, it should worship you, not you worshiping it. But if your mind is darkened with sin, you will do absurd things. The mind is darkened! You can't make the right choices!

Sorcery

Do you listen to the psychic hotline which is nothing but satanic counsel. You listen to Satan for advice and also astrologers and Ouija boards, and tarot cards, and wizards and witches.

The word sorcery comes from the Greek word *pharmasutiko*, where we get our word *pharmacy*. Pharmaceuticals have to do with drugs. If you indulge in sorcery, you get on potions and go into trances. You may eat herbs and other foods of this nature. Do you remember Jim Jones in 1978, he had his followers drink poison that was mixed with Kool-aid. When your mind is blind, you will do anything.

Hatred

Is any person who possess evil intent in your heart toward another person

Variance

Variant people don't like to see any peace. They like to raise hell. They are contentious folk.

Jealousy

Jealousy means anytime you hear about someone else's success, there's a feeling inside of you that makes you angry at what they have. What's the problem? You start comparing yourself. There are people who are so jealous that even though they have a nice car, when they see somebody with a Lexus, they get in debt to buy one. They can't even pay for the one they have.

Jealousy and Wrath

People who are angry don't care if they vent their feelings. They express their anger verbally and if you push them too far, they may express it with their behavior. Selfish ambition, they want to be out front. They want to have the notoriety.

Dissension

When a person is causing confusion, party spirits, and cliques. Heresy is when a person has an opinion and their opinion is right to the contrary of the teachings of the Word of God. They refuse to adjust their opinion to the Word of God—their opinion has to be right.

Drunkenness

If you're a Christian, never let anything control you. When you're drunk, you're out of control. Or, as others might say, you're inebriated. The Christian is never to be under the control of any influence other than the Holy Spirit. Drunkenness.

What do you look like, as a Christian, walking down the street drunk? Can't get out of the car. When people are drunk, they say things they didn't want to tell you— they just couldn't tell you when they were sober. They get bold because the liquor makes them bold. Robbery. People who steal.

Those who practice such deeds shall not enter into the kingdom of God. Characteristics of an unsaved man. He's lost, on his way to hell. God's trying to save him, but he doesn't want to hear it. He wants to go his own way; he doesn't know that it leads to death.

If you stand a guilty distance from God, you need to get right with Him. You need to make a decision this day: You're going to live for Him. The Bible says, when you do that, you hear His word, believe it, and you repent of your sins.

Do you know what repentance means? The word repentance comes from the Greek word *mentaneo*, Which means, "a new mind." *Mata* with *neo* means mind, a new mind. When you repent, God changes your mind; God gives you a new mind. You repent of the old things that you've done, and now you begin to live a new life.

You have decided that you're going to live for him. You confess what you've repented. Confess that Jesus is the Lord of your life. Confessing means to agree with God for without Him, you're lost. You can't earn your salvation, you cannot be smart enough, you cannot buy it. It's a gift freely given. Then not only must you confess, but you must show evidence of your obedience by being buried in the liquid tomb of baptism.

Contrary to popular opinion, baptism is a washing away of one's sins. Baptism is going down into the water and coming up out of the water. Baptism is the death of the old man and the beginning of a new life. Baptism is an operation that God does on your heart. He changes your mind. He changes your condition. He changes your disposition. You can become a new person in Christ.

CHAPTER FOUR

THE
RENEWING
OF THE MIND

We started out in the first chapter talking about the spiritual warfare taking place in the spiritual realm, as well as in the natural realm, between the forces of good and the forces of evil, between the righteousness of God and demonic power.

In the seventh chapter of the book of Romans, Paul talked about how he is in this struggle; he's in this warfare. He knows what the law of God is. The law of God is all of God's will and expectations for his life. Then he says, the law of sin. The law of sin is that which is the opposite of God's will. It is to allow one's own fleshly desires to rule and to reign in a person's life.

Then he said, this war is between the law of God and the law of sin taking place in the law of His mind. The mind is the arena. The mind is neutral and whoever controls the mind controls the law of your members— your physical body.

In other words, your physical body will carry out the wishes of your mind. So Paul said there is a warfare between the law of God and the law of sin taking place in the law of my mind and the law of my members.

Then Paul said, in verse 7:24, "O *wretched man that I am, who will set me free from this body of death. Thanks be to God through Jesus Christ our Lord. So, then, on the one hand I myself with my mind, am serving the Lord God, but on the other, with my flesh, the law of sin.*"

So, we're in this spiritual battle between righteousness and evil, between God and Satan. We've talked about your belief system, because what you believe controls your behavior. It controls how you act, it controls what you think, and it controls what you say.

Then we talked about not only your belief system, but also Biblical characteristics of an unsaved mind. What does an unsaved mind look like as it relates to God? God says the unsaved mind is reprobate.

If man refuses to acknowledge God, God gives him over to a reprobate mind. His mind is corrupt, his mind is twisted and depraved, and, therefore, you don't expect unsaved people to think righteously. Because unsaved people's minds are depraved, unrighteous, corrupt and vain, you do not accept unsaved people's advice.

Psalm 1 says, *"Blessed is the man who walketh not in the counsel of the ungodly nor standing in the way of the sinners nor sitting in the seat of the scornful, but his delight is in the law of the Lord and in His law does he meditate day and night."* Do not go to ungodly, unsaved people for advice. You always go to the Word of God, because the Word of God shapes your belief system, and if it shapes your belief system, it will shape your behavior.

All of us have been created by God, designed by God, and if God designed us, God has a specific way as to how we function. When General Motors creates a car, the auto designers create a car for the purpose of that automobile functioning as it designed to operate.. If it doesn't perform as it is supposed to, you take it back.

I believe that God has made no defect. Whatever God has made is good but because of sin in our lives, sin has messed us up. And many of us are not living on the level that God intends for us to live because of sin.

Romans 12 says, *"Therefore, I urge you brethren, and by the mercies of God that you present your bodies as a living holy sacrifice acceptable to God, which is your spiritual service of worship, and do not be conformed to this world, but be transformed by the renewing of your mind so that you may prove what is the will of God, that which is good and acceptable and perfect."*

First of all, you need to understand that your mind, before you came to Christ, was programmed with unscriptural ideas and thoughts. Your parents told you certain things. Your teachers told you certain things. Your peers told you certain things. The music that you listened to told you certain things.

You have a conscious and a subconscious. Your conscious mind receives information directly, and ,based on what you believe to be true or not true, it is then sent to your subconscious mind. Therefore, your subconscious mind becomes the autopilot. In other words, it becomes your belief system. Therefore, every decision you make is based not on the conscious mind but on the subconscious mind. Why? Because you have been programmed to think a certain way.

The conscious mind receives directions to a friend's home and you've never been there before. You do your best to follow those instructions, making sure you get to the right street, to the right destination.

When you get there, you finally discover where your friend lives. But once you have learned in the conscious mind where he lives, that information is then sent to the subconscious mind, where it is stored.

So, from here on, you do not have directions how to get to his house because you have already been there the first time. You followed directions based on the conscious mind. So now when you go the next time, you do not need directions. You go based on your subconscious mind. It tells you exactly how to get there.

Let me give you another good example. When you learned how to drive, you got in the car and put both hands on the steering wheel. You even turned the radio down. You didn't want any distractions.

But once you learned how to drive, you not only have the radio on, but you talk on the cell phone as you are operating that car based on the subconscious mind. The devil has programmed your mind with old behavior, old patterns, old concepts, old ideas.

When a Christian woman is looking for a husband, God has already told you in His Word in I Timothy 3:1: *"This is the faithful saying, if a man desires the office of a bishop, he desires a good work. A bishop then must be blameless, the husband of one wife. He must be temperate, he must be sober- minded. He must have good behavior and he must be hos-pitable and able to teach. Not given to wine or violence."*

Paul laid out specific behavior as to what you should look for when you seek a leader. Doesn't it make sense that if God wants a specific kind of person to be a leader in the church, shouldn't you look for a person who meets those kinds of qualifications? Look for a man who is a one-woman man.

My point is that if Christian people want to hang out with non-Christian people, you begin to adopt their value systems, their ideas, and their ways of the world rather than renewing your mind.

God wants you to change your mind. In Galatians 5:17, *"For the flesh lusts against the spirit. And the spirit lusts against the flesh." These are contrary to the spirit. If you are led by the spirit, you are not under the law. The works of the flesh are evident."*

When you're in the world, you don't have a problem with committing adultery. When you're in the world, you don't have a problem with committing fornication. You just live the way you choose.

Lewdness

There are people who have no public decency. If what you wear in the bedroom, you wear to the grocery store, you don't have any decency. You will let it all hang out. I'm talking about men and women. You see young men walking down the street with pants halfway down to show their underwear. Nobody wants to see your underwear.

Idolatry

These people worshiped idols. Sorcery. There are people who listen to Cleo. The psychic hotlines and familiar spirits. I'm not surprised when people want to speak to somebody from the dead. They are not talking with anybody from the dead. They're talking to a familiar spirit. A demon will talk in the voice of the person you're trying to reach. Don't think that it's not real.

America has been so Westernized that we

don't think situations like that happen, but you live in a spiritual world, Satan, the god of this world.

Hatred

There are people who hate. You do not like other people for some particular reason. The philosophy is to look out for number one. You put your agenda over other people's agenda's You want to be out front, you want to be the leader.

Christ's model of leadership is that we become servants. We looked at what an unsaved mind looks like, how an unsaved mind needs to renew his mind.

Ideas are reinforced daily and they go virtually unchallenged for many years. Paul said in II Corinthians 10:4, some of these ideas and beliefs are strongholds. A stronghold is a habit that you cannot control. It has power over you. When an enemy has a stronghold on your life, do you know what he does? He fights change.

A stronghold is where an enemy has a position and he uses that position as an advantage, as a leverage, to fight. And whenever the devil gets a foothold in your life, he is not going to let that stronghold go without a fight! That's why it takes prayer and the power of the Holy Spirit to change your life.

Paul said, *"Don't give the devil an opportunity. Don't give him any place in your life."* When you give him an inch, he'll take a whole yard. And then, the next thing you know, the person who is calling the shots in your life is not you, but the devil.

Ephesians 2:1, says *"And which He made alive who were dead in your trespasses and in your sin. In which you once walked according to the course of this world."* According to the *prince and power of the air,* Satan controlled your life.

The spirit who now is at work and in the sons of disobedience. When you see people breaking the law, they will not live long. The way of the transgressor is hard. If you sow to the flesh, you reap the things of the flesh.

When a concept or idea becomes a part of your thinking process, it will always lead you to the same predetermined conclusion. The way you see the world is based on your belief system. It will determine how you will treat others. Since you are in Christ, your decision-making cannot be based on old information stored in your subconscious mind, but upon the Word of God.

II Corinthians 5:17, says, *"If any man is in Christ, he is a new creature, old things are passed away and behold all things have become new."* When Christ came into your life, your thinking changes. But the only way you can change your thinking is to have your mind renewed by the power of the Holy Spirit.

Through the power of the Spirit, God gives you a new mind. In Jeremiah 17, He talks about giving Israel a new heart. God can write His law, not upon tables of stone, but He can write His laws upon your heart.

In Romans 8, Paul talked about you what you look like in Christ. Paul said that he couldn't keep the law of God because the law of sin was always present. There is a warfare between the law of my mind and the law of my members. He goes on to say, "Oh, *wretched man that I am, who will deliver me from this body of death?"*

In Romans 8:1, Paul said *"There is no condemnation to those who are in Christ."* I want you to know that you are in Christ and if you are in Christ, there is no condemnation. There is no judgment of the wrath of God upon your life because you have surrendered and submitted your life to the will of God.

Do not walk according to the flesh but walk according to the spirit. Your flesh has to do with your sense of knowledge. Sense knowledge is what you hear, see, smell, taste, and touch. We call these the five senses. Sometimes a person may say something that doesn't make sense. People will say, "Well, he's smart but he just doesn't have common sense."

The Christian should practice and do things that do not make common sense. If you're not walking after the flesh and walking after the spirit, it doesn't make any common sense, but it's uncommon.

Paul said, the Christian should not walk by flesh but walk by the Spirit. If you want to walk by the Spirit, you're going to have to walk by the word. If you do not know the word, you cannot walk by the Spirit.

So, if you want to have your mind changed, you're going to have to begin with the word. When you begin with the word, the Holy Spirit takes the Word and begins to apply it to your life.

If you follow the law of the Spirit, then the law of the Spirit will make you free from the law of sin. In your nature, there is a principle law called "sin" that wants to bring you down, take you opposite of God's will.

But when you're in Christ, you have the law of the spirit, which produces life, sets you free from the law of sin and death. *What the law could not do in that it was weak through the flesh, God did it by sending Jesus, in the likeness of sinful flesh.*

In other words, God sent Jesus to be our example. He paid the price. As long as you trust Jesus, as long as you stay in Him, then

He says He will change you. By His life, by His example, He met the requirements of the law and He produced in us the righteousness that we could not produce by ourselves.

So, if you're righteous, there is no condemnation. Those who are in Christ's body are not condemned, but they are justified before God. If you have the righteousness of God in your life, then, you should not be living a defeated life.

In Romans 5:12-21, Paul said that death reigned in Adam. That is, all of us died as a result of Adam's sin. But because of Jesus, you reign in life.

If you are reigning with Christ, you ought to be ruling and reigning and have control of your life. And if circumstances occur, you do not let circumstances dictate to you in terms of the quality of faith you have.

God's power has the ability to keep us, even in the midst of danger, doubt, and discouragement. He's able to keep us. But many people believe the answer is not in Christ, but out there in the world.

They'll never be able to be what God wants them to be because they're not living the way God wants them to. They want to find the right answers to life, but they're looking for the right answers in the wrong place. They're not going to find them there. You find answers to life's questions only in God's word.

In Romans 12:1-2, it tells how to renew your mind. *"I beseech you brother by the mercies of God that you present your body."* This is your physical body. Surrender your physical body as a living sacrifice. What's a sacrifice? You put a sacrifice on an altar. Your body becomes your sacrifice. You give your body to God. Make sure you are acceptable unto God.

In the Old Testament, in the book of Leviticus 5, God did not accept any kind of sacrifice. God didn't accept sacrifices that were blemished. If there was a lamb or a goat that was maimed, God did not receive it.

You have Christians maiming their bodies, torturing their bodies, cutting their bodies, tattooing their bodies. Your body doesn't belong to you. If it doesn't belong to you, do you have the right to cut it up, mark it up? It belongs to Jesus.

Paul said, in I Corinthians 6, *"Therefore, your body is a temple of the Holy Spirit."* If the body is a temple of the Holy Spirit, you should be disciplined enough to take care of your body. Rest, eat right, exercise. It's about renewing the mind. If you want to lose weight, you think you can eat chocolate cake? You need to learn to quit being flesh walkers and be spirit walkers. We walk by the spirit. We're letting this body control us. We need to control it! That's what it means to renew the mind. It means lifestyle changes.

I discovered the reason why we can't give any more to the church, to support the church. We're broke because of our lifestyles. You make choices at the mall that you can't afford. God has a way for you to live. God doesn't intend for us to be stressed out, not having any money.

Biblical Meditation

God has a way of helping you to change your mind through meditation.

In Joshua 1:1-9:

"The servant of the Lord, it came to pass, that the Lord spoke unto Joshua, the son of Nun, saying, Moses, my servant, is dead. Now then, arise and go over Jordan, you and all of these people, to the land I'm giving unto them, to the children of Israel. Every place that the sole of your foot shall trod I have given unto you. And I said unto Moses, from the wilderness unto Lebanon, to the great river, the river Euphrates. All of the land of the Hittites to the going down of the sun shall be yours! Territory. No man will be able to stand before you all the days of your life. As I was with Moses, so will I be with you. I will not leave you nor forsake you. Be strong. Be of good courage for thus people you shall divide as an inheritance that land which I have sworn to your fathers. Only be strong

and courageous that you do that you observe. According to all of the law."

If you're going to be successful and be what God wants you to be, you have to observe His will. Why? Because God's will is your direction. His Word is your map. The Word is your blueprint to build your life.

Who would build a house if they do not have blueprints? The house must be built according to architectural design and codes. Why is that? Right now, everything's fine. But there is a point where meteorologists call storm season. It is predictable you're going to have storms.

So, if you want to be ready when the storms come, you cannot start building in a storm. But a lot of people start trying to build in the midst of a storm.

Jesus said, *"If you do not build your house on the rock when the storms come, floods come, winds come, blow and beat on your life, you will not stand."* Why? Because you're not prepared. The only way you will be prepared, you must have your mind changed. He says, the law, the Word of God, is a blueprint, a map.

Joshua, do not depart neither from the right hand nor to the left. That you may prosper. God wants you to prosper! Then why are you not prospering? Prosperity is not where you are. Prosperity is on you! Why is prosperity on you? Because you are connected to the divine source. Jesus said, *"Seek first the kingdom of heaven and it righteousness. All of these things will be added unto you."* You're connected to the source.

This book of the law shall not depart from your mouth. If you read the Word of God, it says that *the book of the law shall not depart from your mouth.* That means you have to confess the word. That means you've got to talk the word.

The book of the law shall not depart from your mouth. You must learn to speak the word. When your children are ungodly, just say, "Lord, in the name of Jesus, I'm praying for these children." "My husband will not do right. Lord, I'm praying, change him! Based not on what I want but on what you want."

If you do not know the word, how are you going to speak over your situation with the words that you need to speak? Meditate in the book, day and night, every day. Constantly. You know why? Because the Bible said, in II Corinthians 10:3-4, the devil always shoots thoughts in your mind, and the only way you can cast down imaginations is knowing the word.

When Jesus was tempted, in Matthew 4, *"That man shall not live by bread alone, but every word that proceeds out of the mouth God."* Jesus had to quote scripture to defeat the devil. How will you defeat him if you do not know the word? Meditate day and night.

Philippians 4:7 says, *"Let the peace of God, which surpasses all understanding, regulate your heart and your mind."* Then peace of God will protect your mind from the anxieties of this world. The reason why you are stressed out is because you have no peace. *"Brethren, whatever things are true are noble, just, pure, lovely, and of good report. If there's anything praiseworthy, meditate on these thoughts."*

The reason why you cannot produce the positive things in your life is because you're meditating on the wrong things. In Proverbs 4:23, Solomon said, *"Keep your heart with all diligence for out of it flows the issues of life."*

What you think about the most is what you do. Whatever constantly bombards your mind or bombards your thinking eventually you will begin to do it. That's why, when a thought comes from the devil, you must capture it, you must immediately reject it. Your mind has been programmed to the flesh.

If you begin to reprogram your mind with the Word of God, meditate, think about it constantly, read it, pray it, speak it, confess it, live it. And guess what? You will change.

Michael Jordan became the greatest basketball player, or one of the greatest basketball players who ever lived. Why? It's not because, at game time, he was able to do outstanding feats. This was not his success. His success was in practice.

So, when the time came for him to succeed, or rise to the occasion, he knew what his body could do. He knew what he had been practicing all the time. So, I'm saying to you, the secret to being able to renew your mind and to live as God wants you live and to walk as God wants you to walk is to read God's Word in your private time. When temptations come at you, you can say, in the name of Jesus, I reject them.

When you hear people talk about defeatism and you hear people say "Oh, I'm sad and depressed," you can reject that and just say, "Not me." You refuse to let other people's depression affect you. Some people talk about negativity, you do not want to be around them, especially when there is a way to change how you think.

The world bases its value system on how you look, how much money you have, what you drive, and where you live. Your identity in Christ is based on who you are in Christ. So, if you are a new creature, you do not allow old ways of thinking, old patterns, old habits, old concepts, old friends dictate to you. This is the struggle. If you really want your life to be different, you must begin to take God's Word seriously and allow His spirit to live in you.

OTHER BOOKS BY DR. KENNETH GILMORE

Leadership In African American
Churches of Christ

The New Covenant: Your Rights and
Privileges

What Is Biblical Faith?

How To Have Success With God

Bring Me The Book

The Apostle's Doctrine

Money: God's Financial Plan For Your Life

Unmasking Satanic Lies

The Authority of The Believer

Principle Centered Living

The Power of The Tongue

Prayer, The Key To Success

God's Spiritual Laws

What Kind of Man Are You

The Decision Is in Your Hand

~

TAPE SERIES BY DR. KENNETH GILMORE

New Covenant: Your Rights	2 Tapes
What Is Biblical Faith?	2 Tapes
How To Have Success With God	5 Tapes
Money: God's Financial Plan	2 Tapes
Unmasking Satanic Lies	2 Tapes
The Authority of The Believer	4 Tapes
The Power of The Tongue	3 Tapes
God's Spiritual Laws	6 Tapes
What Kind of Man Are You?	3 Tapes
Principle Centered Living	3 Tapes
The New Testament Church, Which One Is True?	2 Tapes
The Battle For The Mind	4 Tapes
Prayer	4 Tapes

BECOME A COVENANT TRUTH PARTNER WITH KENNETH GILMORE MINISTRIES!

Because of the power that comes through fellowship, commitment and partnership, we invite you to join with Dr. Kenneth Gilmore in fulfilling the vision God has given him. Dr. Gilmore has been given a mandate to teach the Word of God in simple terms so that all can understand.

It's easy to become a Covenant Truth Partner. Simply fill out the form on page 101 and mail it to:

Kenneth Gilmore Ministries
3615 SW 13th Street
Gainesville, FL 32641

Our prayer for you is that as you enter covenant with us, God's blessings and mani-fold riches will be unleashed in your life.

Covenant Truth Partners have sought the Lord and received His confirmation of the worth of this ministry. Therefore, Partners are more than friends, they are loyal, trusted allies in the ministry. We value all of our Covenant Truth Partners and hold them up to God in prayer, minister to them with a personal monthly letter and offer from time to time dis-counted products for spiritual edification and growth.

THERE IS VALUE IN COVENANT TRUTH PARTNERSHIP!

Yes. I'd like to become a Covenant Truth Partner in prayer and financial support with Kenneth Gilmore Ministries.

_____
Last Name

_____
First Name   Middle Initial

_____
Street Address   Apartment No.

_____
City   State   Zip

You can count on me for a monthly pledge of:

❑ $1,000   ❑ $500   ❑ $100

❑ $50   ❑ $25   ❑ $_____

❑ One time gift of $_____

PERSONAL NOTES

PERSONAL NOTES

PERSONAL NOTES

www.ingramcontent.com/pod-product-compliance
Lightning Source LLC
Chambersburg PA
CBHW051840040426
42447CB00006B/628